Joey Chestnut's America

Politics, Patriotism and the Future of Democracy

William W. Sokoloff

Copyright © 2025 William W. Sokoloff
All rights reserved

ISBN: 979-8-9921594-3-1

Cover Artwork by José Ramón Lerma

Interior Artwork by Emilio Villalba

Author Photo by Kerry Daly Sokoloff

San Francisco, California

Dedicated to my father, William J. Sokoloff

INTRODUCTION

In June of 1870, Congress made Independence Day on the Fourth of July a federal holiday. Via a legislative act, Congress linked a precise historical moment in the past to a yearly celebration in the present and future. Since then, a variety of practices take place to celebrate American independence including gatherings with friends and family, picnics and pyrotechnic events. Every Fourth of July since 1916, Nathan's Hotdogs (a brand and food product currently under the umbrella of Smithfield Foods) has sponsored a hot dog eating contest on Coney Island, New York. Since the 1970s, it has been televised. Over the years, I heard about the hot dog eating contest. When I watched it on television, it was painful to observe but it was difficult to look away. In 2023, Joey "JAWS" Chestnut ate 62 hot dogs and buns in 10 minutes.[1] The proud holder of the "Mustard Belt," Chestnut has won the contest sixteen times (2007-2014 and 2016-2023). In fifteen contests, he is estimated to have eaten 142 pounds of beef hot dogs.

It is easy to view Chestnut's competitive eating as a freakish and grotesque form of American nihilism. One that links patriotism with manic consumption. If this is the case, we can turn away with disgust. But there is more to the story than this. Competitive eating, a previously underground practice, became a public spectacle that raises questions about agency, self-negation, masculinity, sexuality and other serious issues. The fact that the United States's population is one of the most obese on the globe has not diminished interest in competitive eating.

What do the rising popularity of competitive eating events and Joey Chestnut say about politics, patriotism and American democracy? A book that asks these questions doesn't exist. I seek to fill a gap in the discourse about competitive eating and Joey Chestnut that connects his emergence in the public spotlight with major shifts in the realm of politics. My argument is not that Chestnut embodies the excesses of our time including ones found in

---

[1] For the challenge of fitting something large inside oneself see St. Augustine: "What room is there in me for my God"; *Confessions*, translator Sheed, (Indianapolis, IN: Hackett Press, 1992), p. 3.

the realm of politics. Nor is it that Chestnut is the dark side of the American dream. Rather, it is that American democracy has become a deranged entertainment regime. The American public seems to know that not much will change from electoral politics. Given that, the public supports candidates who command the national media-microphone, insult political enemies and espouse a symbolic commitment to the American way of life, even if the candidate's policy proposals go against their economic interests. Analyzing Joey Chestnut's rise provides a way to understand the transformation of American politics into an entertainment regime beyond the standard corporate-oligarchic critique. Approaching politics via Chestnut leads to a new way of understanding politics but also opens paths for agency beyond the arguments about working class false consciousness, pessimistic conclusions about corporate domination and the rise of Christo-fascism.[2]

In terms of the methodology of what follows, there isn't one in any of the conventional forms. I approach Chestnut and American politics with a critically informed, interpretive and nonsectarian mindset. One suited to the chaos and heart attack rhythms of the American absurdist entertainment machine. My approach requires disruptive perspective changing that crashes incompatible discourses into each other. One that confuses high and low, sacred and profane, beautiful and ugly and political versus non-political. Nor is there any over-arching theoretical framework that organizes everything about Chestnut, connects it to American politics, then spits it out in a pragmatic take-away.[3] This type of approach isn't suited to the contemporary political moment.

If Donald J. Trump's rise to power has taught us anything, it is that democracy is not based on deliberation and reason. Contra Aristotle, the human is not always a political animal but one

---

[2] For an analysis of these themes see William E. Connolly, *Aspirational Fascism: The Struggle for Multifaceted Democracy Under Trumpism* (Minneapolis, MN: University of Minnesota Press, 2017).

[3] For an appeal for the left to be pragmatic see Richard Rorty, *Achieving Our Country: Leftist Thought in Twentieth Century America* (Cambridge, MA: Harvard University Press, 1999).

frequently dominated by their appetites and passions. Trump knows how to talk to people in ways they understand even if what he says is complete nonsense (e.g., Haitian immigrants eating pets; transgender takeover in prisons and schools; undocumented criminal immigrant invasion; DEI causing planes to crash). In the current moment, electoral politics has become a noisy monster truck jam and a world wrestling federation spectacle where rational argumentation is impossible. It is what seems crazy and irrational that seems to work in the realm of American democratic politics. As an example, Trump's supporters love his self-aggrandizing rants, fantasies of persecution and against-all-odds legal victories. His belligerence does not make people recoil but intensifies the applause. His incoherent speeches, arm-jerk dancing and absurd public statements successfully sold his political brand of greatness to white nationalists, tech billionaires, Christian evangelicals and disgruntled working people.

What should the progressive left do? A new approach to political mobilization is needed. The left needs to exploit and navigate the new absurdity-entertainment-misinformation-nonsense nexus. Of course, the minimum wage, access to quality education and healthcare matter for most Americans. Straight talk about these issues is not how one wins an election. Absurdity, disruption and humor are the new weapons of politics. For the progressive left, absurdity, disruption and humor can overturn hierarchies, desecrate authoritarian institutions and fill the world with joy and laughter.[4] Laughter disrupts the uncritical circulation of bodies, commodities and ideas. Low brow comical popular culture that reverses high and low and fucks shit up can open new utopian horizons and expand the democratic imagination beyond Marxist critique, endless deconstruction, mainstream electoral politics and other forms of moralizing. It is time to embrace anarchy and chaos, make a mess,

---

[4] For these and related themes see Mikhail Bakhtin, *Rabelais and his World*, translated by Hélène Iswolsky, (Bloomington, IN: Indiana University Press, 2009).

be disruptive, exploit the spectacle of politics, promote nonsense and experiment with making politics something hilarious.[5]

---

[5] I agree with Frances Fox Piven about the value of disruption for democratic politics. See *Challenging Authority: How Ordinary People Change America* (New York, NY: Rowman & Littlefield, 2006).

1

To understand the importance of hotdog eating contests and the connection to American democracy, competitive eating should be situated within a broader historical context. The American colonial experience that culminated in severing political ties with the British Crown impacted basic aspects of everyday life. Armed with the doctrine formal equality, Americans prided themselves on the rejection of British snobbery. This played out in the creation of new political institutions but also impacted American dress and food consumption mores.[6] In terms of clothing, casual attire won the day. In terms of eating, Americans ate on the go, while walking, standing up and ate in public spaces. Overeating became the norm. Political and cultural differences but also economic instability of life in the colonies contributed to a distinctly American way of eating. Eating competitions premised on the rejection of European refinement served not only cultural and entertainment but political objectives too.

Food consumption mores were not only about looking back at England and asserting a unique American identity but managing internal power relations at home. In the United States, eating contests were deployed by whites as a source of racial entertainment. In the American context, racial entertainment can be defined as staged performances that perpetuate assumptions about African American inferiority. Americans found the staged humiliation and subjugation of previously enslaved persons amusing. Like the low sports referenced by Frederick Douglass in his autobiographies to make enslaved persons hate freedom and entertain slave masters, gorging competitions between African Americans perpetuated racial power. As Itai Vardi argues, "food was used to stereotype blacks." Competitive food eating contests, Vardi continues, "constituted specialized sites in which powerful white actors sought to delineate group boundaries along racial lines as part of a broader remapping of power structures during the post-

---

[6] See Alexis de Tocqueville, *Democracy in America*, translated by George Lawrence, (New York, NY: Perennial Classics, 2000).

Reconstruction era."⁷ In 1894, the New York City police department hosted a pie eating contest between African Americans.⁸ Racialized eating competitions confirmed beliefs about the animality of African Americans and justified continued domination, exclusion and marginalization after the partial juridical prohibition on slavery in the 13th Amendment. As the twentieth century marched along, these and other racist practices had to take more coded forms as the doctrine of color blindness became common currency.⁹ Even if certain groups continue to be marked as eating and liking foods that pertain to their identity and race, eating competitions lost the explicit racial aspect. The need to regulate food competition events as well as broader interest in food eating competitions led to the creation of the International Federation of Competitive Eating [IFCE] in 1997. National and international live broadcasts of the competitions are now common. Rivalries between competitors piqued public interest. In 2007, the reigning hotdog eating champion Takera Kobayashi was dethroned by Joey Chestnut. The star power of Kobayashi and Chestnut set the stage for an explosion of popular interest in competitive eating.

---

⁷ See Itai Vardi, "Feeding Race: Eating Contests, the Black Body, and the Social Production of Group Boundaries through Amusement in turn of the Twentieth Century America," *Food, Culture & Society*, 13:3, (Sept. 2010): 5, 1.
⁸ Vardi, 2010, 4-5. Food eating contests between African Americans occurred as late as 1928.
⁹ For these and related themes see Ian Haney López, *Dog Whistle Politics: How Coded Racial Appeals Have Reinvented Racism and Wrecked the Middle Class* (New York, NY: Oxford University Press, 2015).

2

Joey Chestnut was born on November 25, 1983, in Fulton County, Kentucky. He currently lives in an upscale area near Indianapolis, Indiana. He is 6'1 and weighs 230 pounds. Chestnut attended San Jose State University. The rise of Joey Chestnut into the national and international spotlight has been a protracted process. A turning point was his victory over the reigning Japanese hot dog eating champion Takeru "Tsunami" Kobayashi in 2007 thus restoring US global supremacy. Hot dogs are not the only thing Chestnut eats in competitive food eating events. In 2013, Chestnut ate one hundred forty-one hard boiled eggs in eight minutes. In 2009, Chestnut ate Iguana's Burritozilla, a five pound, 17-inch burrito in roughly three minutes. On May 8, 2010, Chestnut ate 380 wontons in eight minutes. On September 2, 2012, Chestnut consumed 191 wings in 12 minutes to win the 1st place competitive-eating trophy at the National Buffalo Wing Contest in Buffalo, New York.[10] Recently, he ate twenty pounds of shrimp.

In terms of visibility, Chestnut appeared on the twelfth episode of Hell's Kitchen, Season 10. In 2020, Chestnut guest starred on the animated series Scooby Doo and Guess Who?[11] Chestnut's sponsors include PepsiCo, Dude Wipes, Raising Canes and Wonderful Pistachios. Chestnut's net worth is estimated to be four million dollars. In terms of political connections, Joey Chestnut was the official food taster for President Donald Trump.[12] Recently, Chestnut did not compete in Nathan's 2024 hotdog contest.

---

[10] See James Brown, *Hungry for Glory the Joey Chestnut Story: Devouring the World One Bite at a Time*, (Coppell, TX: James Brown, 2024), pp. 26-38.

[11] See https://en.wikipedia.org/wiki/Joey_Chestnut (accessed April 18, 2024).

[12] See Allen Ishac, "Trump Will Be First U.S. President to Have Personal Food Taster," Medium.com, January 26, 2017. https://allanishac.medium.com/trump-taps-joey-chestnut-to-be-personal-food-taster-69fcfadb0e85, (accessed April 17, 2024).

3

The cultural, historical, political and racial dynamics circling around competitive eating are difficult to miss. Chestnut is wrapped up in the cultural and political spotlight with a high-profile television appearance on one of the few national holidays in the US. He is also courted by a populist president and sponsored by major corporations. He recently signed a contract with Net Flix estimated to be worth 10 million dollars. Public fascination with him continues to increase. Treating him as an object of political and theoretical analysis is not easy. In writing this piece, I struggled with how to approach him. How much and what can one say about someone who stuffs themselves to the breaking point with hotdogs? Chestnut resists political interpretation because he is not political in any obvious way.

In what follows, I treat the competitive hotdog eating champion Joey Chestnut as a complicated anti-aesthetic text to interpret in relation to American politics and the crisis of the leftist imagination. I draw on a variety of scholarly sources to decipher Chestnut including comparisons with pornography, queer and anarchist theory as well as radical democratic theory. I am particularly interested in the use of Chestnut's whole person as a patriotic celebration of American greatness that results in his self-destruction. As James C. Scott argues, self-negation can be a political act when there are no other options.[13] Via an analysis of his body, facial gestures, person, mouth and belly, Chestnut provides an opportunity to interrogate a variety of political concepts and reflect on the current state of American politics, the politics of spectacle and the crisis of patriarchal masculinity while also engaging the antisocial thesis in queer theory. As we shall see, performance art, even forms

---

[13] See James C. Scott, *Domination and the Arts of Resistance: Hidden Transcripts* (New Haven, CT: Yale University Press, 1992). For an analysis of self-starvation as resistance on a slave ship see Saidiya Hartman, *Losing Your Mother: A Journey Along the Atlantic Slave Route* (New York, NY: Farrar, Straus and Giroux, 2007).

of it that stretch the meaning of the word, have liberatory and revolutionary potential.[14]

---

[14] For the liberatory and revolutionary potential of art see Herbert Marcuse, *The Aesthetic Dimension: Toward a Critique of Marxist Aesthetics* (Boston, MA: Beacon Press, 1979). See also Jill Dolan on the utopian significance of performance in *Utopia in Performance: Finding Hope at the Theater* (Ann Arbor, MI: University of Michigan Press, 2005).

4

The ideas and themes covered in this chapter are uncomfortable. Aesthetically, Chestnut eating hot dogs on an international ESPN televisual broadcast has a strange backyard and garage feel to it. Because of how the competition is staged on an elevated table, one can sense a "Last Supper" vibe but with patriotic flair given the American flags. The Christian aspect operates alongside a transgressive sexual one. Analogous to the crime scene ambience of 1970s and 1980s sexual cinematic culture where there is groaning, flesh, yoga contortions to facilitate sexual intercourse in different poses, drooling, slurping, heavy breathing and a variety of dilated and gaping bodily orifice, competitive eating is similarly arresting to watch.[15] One sees what was previously forbidden to see. Raw, authentic and real, competitive eating events satisfy the hunger viewers have for shocking experiences where humans push themselves to the breaking point. Bodies, hands, mouths and throats are on stage. During the competitive eating event, the mouth serves as a highway for hot dogs and other food.

Estimated to gross between fifteen to ninety-seven billion a year in the US, porn consumption dwarfs the interest and money in competitive eating events. However, both share some things in common beyond the issues already flagged. I am not interested in the connection to pornography to echo the standard critique of it as a form of compensation for the powerlessness of heterosexual men via the fantasy of unlimited sexual availability of the female body for their pleasure. Nor does the standard feminist critique of porn as the dehumanization and objectification of young women pertain to my argument.[16] It is the realist aesthetic and superhuman gymnastics of pornography and competitive eating that interests me. Like a porn star, Chestnut is an athlete who has compared himself to the boxer

---

[15] For the attraction and repulsion dynamic of the monster, see Judith Halberstam, *Skin Shows: Gothic Horror and the Technology of Monsters* (Durham, NC: Duke University Press, 1995).

[16] For these and related themes pertaining to the cruelty and violence of pornography see Andrea Dworkin, *Heartbreak: The Political Memoir of a Militant Feminist* (New York, NY: Basic Books, 2002).

Mike Tyson. As with porn, "extreme eating shows the body at work without restraint and without interference."[17] During the food consumption act, Chestnut operates at a compulsive and manic pace, feeding hotdogs into his mouth, stuffing more in, dipping them into water as a lubricant, throating them down and pushing himself beyond limits. He performs what Linda Williams calls the "frenzy of the visible."[18] Tantamount to the experience of wonder, the frenzy of the visible in porn disrupts routinization and provides an experience of shock designed to sexually arouse the viewer. As Chestnut eats and inhales hotdogs at the Nathan's Fourth of July event, the obvious sexual connection would be to a patriotic form of *fellatio*, albeit with a non-ejaculating hot dog. The porn classic *Deep Throat* (1972) only partially applies to Chestnut because, unlike Linda Lovelace, Chestnut does not have a clitoris in his throat. Nevertheless, Chestnut's hot dog eating could be viewed as a sequel to *Deep Throat*.

In contrast to Lovelace, Chestnut swallows disembodied edible phallic surrogates. Exploring the connections between Chestnut and porn provides new ways to interpret both and can be a contribution to the emerging field of critical porn studies.[19] Chestnut arguably sexualizes patriotism in the crisis of heterosexual masculinity. He performs masculinity as the public display of gastronomical transgression, pushing himself beyond limits and taking in more than he can handle.[20] The patriotic side of Chestnut is at least as important as the sexual-social aspect. At the hotdog event, Chestnut puts his life on the line. He does this for America on the Fourth of July by eating more hot dogs than anyone else in ten minutes.

---

[17] See Priscilla Parkhurst Ferguson, "Inside the Extreme Sport of Competitive Eating," *Contexts*, Vol. 13, No. 3 (Summer 2014): 31.

[18] See Linda Williams, *Hard Core: Power, Pleasure and the 'Frenzy of the Visible,'* (Berkeley, CA: University of California Press, 1989).

[19] For an analysis of relationships between politics, masculinity and gay porn, see Tim Dean, *Unlimited Intimacy: Reflections on the Subculture of Barebacking* (Chicago, IL: University of Chicago Press, 2009).

[20] For masculinity as taking in more than one can handle see Dean, *Unlimited Intimacy*, 2009, p. 125.

Beyond the patriotic aspect, there is also a strange form of political agency in play. Namely, one turned inside out, or what I call oxymoronic agency. As a skilled performance artist with a one-man circus act, Chestnut disrupts the manufacturing laboratory of neoliberal subjectivity. If it is true that "self-starvation stages the event of *subjectivation*," as Patrick Anderson argues in *So Much Wasted: Hunger, Performance and the Morbidity of Resistance*, competitive eating stages the collapse of subjectivization.[21] First I shall say a few words about subjectivation. Then I move on to its collapse.

---

[21] See Patrick Anderson, *So Much Wasted: Hunger, Performance, and the Morbidity of Resistance*, (Durham, NC: Duke University Press, 2010), p. 3.

5

Subjectivation constitutes the self to itself as an object of knowledge. As readers of Michel Foucault may recall, people as subjects are produced through disciplinary discourses on normality as an explicitly political demobilization project. Discourses are peddled by dominant institutions (e.g., schools; prisons; family; psychiatrists; workplace) to normalize people into a manageable mass. People are taught to police themselves into acceptable forms of docility.[22] The self learns to perform work on itself via a will to power turned against the instinct for freedom.[23] The self no longer needs the constant presence of an external power (e.g., police officer; prison guard) to beat itself into submission but performs this work on itself. The self becomes an inmate and its own prison guard in the prison it calls freedom.

A prisoner and prison guard but also slave and slave master. Always at work, the self operates under a self-imposed management regime. This includes exercise, dieting, calorie counting, avoiding donuts and fried food and owning a step counting device. The neoliberal subject's goal is a paradoxical form of disciplinary bliss involving its relentless subjection to norms. Physical fitness as an ascetic regime names a path to the maximization of productivity as a coherent brand and over-caffeinated entrepreneur. Physical fitness also positions the subject as a worker ready for overtime exploitation and as an able-bodied soldier ready to kill for their country.

The collapse of subjectivation suspends all of this through modes of self-cancellation. At competitive eating events, Chestnut eats himself into a coma. Immediately after the event, he cannot work, think, sleep, talk and function. Even though he trains for eating events, Chestnut both confirms and exceeds the disciplinary regime of neoliberalism and subjectivation. Chestnut sacrifices

---

[22] See Michel Foucault, *Abnormal: Lectures at the College de France, 1974-1975,* translated by Graham Burchell (New York, NY: Picador, 2003).
[23] For these and related themes see Friedrich Nietzsche, *On the Genealogy of Morals*, translated by Walter Kaufmann and RJ Hollingdale (New York, NY: Vintage Press, 1989).

himself for America but more radically, creating a brand and selling it to anyone interested in buying it but with a nihilistic twist. As a result of the competition, he temporarily incapacitates himself. Bloated, he becomes dysfunctional and shattered. The only things he can do after the hotdog contest are grimace and moan as sixty hotdogs pass through his body. Chestnut thus performs the collapse of subjectivation.

Joey Chestnut is a Christ-like figure, a vessel, an empty signifier and a punk rock martyr. He takes himself to the limits of emptiness. He attaches himself to corporate and political hosts who stand by his side as he desecrates himself for his country. He is apolitical as a circus stuntman who dazzles audiences with over-consumption. Like American politics, Chestnut performs the politics of something unhinged and manic, one on the skids, freakish, derailed and abysmal. And it is in this aspect that a strange utopianism comes into view, one that is dysfunctional to neoliberal subjectivity, militarism and project of national greatness. Via the collapse of subjectivation, Chestnut pushes himself and a bloated empire to its breaking point. Because he is both functional and dysfunctional, Chestnut refuses the available and established cultural and political options that constitute a person as normal. He also breaks with dominant forms of relationality premised on moderation, respecting boundaries and living a life in accordance with the Aristotelian mean. With Chestnut, time stands still. He says with a mouth full of hot dogs but without explicitly saying it, "the future must stop here."[24] Chestnut arrests time in excessive bloating. He collapses linear time and lives on in dead time.[25]

---

[24] Lee Edelman, *No Future: Queer Theory and the Death Drive* (Durham, NC: Duke University Press, 2004), p. 31.

[25] For these and related themes see Judith Halberstam, *In a Queer Time and Place: Transgender Bodies, Subcultural Lives* (New York, NY: New York University Press, 2005). See also Elizabeth Freeman, *Time Binds: Queer Temporalities, Queer Histories* (Durham, NC: Duke University Press, 2010).

6

In *Man Bites Dog: Hot Dog Culture in America*, Bruce Kraig and Patty Carroll argue that the hotdog is an essential aspect of American democracy, interclass contact and street culture.[26] As the modern industrial workforce was constituted via the creation of large-scale manufacturing assembly lines, an over-worked, exploited and disgruntled American working class emerged. Automobile manufacturing plants designed by Henry Ford implemented time management discipline with the ideas of Frederick Winslow Taylor. This increased productivity but also exacerbated human misery and led to environmental devastation. At critical moments of worker unrest, the US federal government intervened to ameliorate militant explosions of class conflict with policies regulating the terms of work (e.g., creation of a weekend; limits on workday; restrictions on child labor) and created national parks as spaces of rejuvenation via communion with nature (the National Park Service was created in 1916). Strangely, the hotdog solved a variety of problems linked to the emergence of an exploited workforce, industrialization and environmental decimation.

Beyond serving as an identity marker for what it meant to be American for a growing number of immigrants, the hotdog made consumption easy since a plate and silverware was not necessary to consume it. It also made caloric consumption efficient. By holding the meat in a bun, one could eat it anywhere. It was also cheap and anticipated the popularity of other hand-held devices. Unlike a beef steak with a bone that carries with it the trace of the animal, the artificial shape and color of the hot dog bare little visible connection to a sentient being. Millions of people love to eat them. For Jacques Derrida, "the moral question is not should one eat or not." For the

---

[26] See Bruce Kraig and Patty Carrol, *Man Bites Dog: Hot Dog Culture in America*, (New York: Taylor Trade Publishing, 2012). For the ethical and political quandaries posed by dogs see Kennan Ferguson, "I Love My Dog," *Political Theory*, 32:3 (Jun. 2004): 373-395.

Algerian assassin of western metaphysics, it is to "eat well."[27] The hotdog, largely through incessant marketing campaigns, technological innovations, the flood of immigrants into American urban centers and disruptions to temporality caused by capitalism became an American staple, a first-generation form of fast food, a way of eating well as an American worker.

---

[27] See Jacques Derrida, "Eating Well, or the Calculation of the Subject," in *Points…Interviews, 1974-1994*, translated by Peggy Kamuf (Stanford, CA: Stanford University Press, 1995), p. 282.

7

During the hotdog competition, Chestnut stands and eats. Chestnut's will to devour the other goes beyond the necessary bounds to sustain life involved in ingesting an animal corpse. Through rigorous pre-competition training, he disciplines himself not to vomit during and after the contest. In a similar way that Kant in *Metaphysics of Morals* criticizes masturbation in the section called "On Defiling Oneself by Lust," and other nonteleological sexual encounters as violating human dignity [*Würde*], Chestnut abuses and uses himself as a means.[28] Eating excessive hotdogs puts a strange twist on Kant's prohibition on defiling oneself by lust. It is difficult to imagine how gorge eating can be pleasurable for the one doing the eating given the obvious side-effects. Chestnut stages his annihilation in an out-of-control form of low-brow competitive consumption as an anti-aesthetic phenomenon that gives non-normative pleasure to the viewers of the event. Fascinated, viewers watch and wait for the surprises promised by gorge eating. As his jaws move up and down, throat flexes, body contorts, all eyes are on Chestnut.

---

[28] See Immanuel Kant, *Metaphysics of Morals*, translated by Mary Gregor (Cambridge, UK: Cambridge University Press, 1990), pp. 220-221.

8

Politics is an elusive object of study. It is also risky business because political order is held together by the widespread belief in its authority. Hence, authority and politics lack a stable foundation.[29] As a historical and public activity that lacks stable ground, politics is more of an art than a science. As art, politics is about the manipulation of appearances. As such, it is a performance and takes place on stage. The best politicians are good actors. Even though they serve the financial interests that back them, politicians must be perceived by the public as serving the common good. Even when they succeed, everything can unexpectedly change. Regimes can crumble in an instant.[30]

Politics is thus the public and staged art of improvisation. Learning how to live is also an art. Nietzsche said, "life is only justified as an aesthetic phenomenon."[31] For Nietzsche, life was nothing more than pain, suffering and existential incomprehensibility.[32] No deeper reality. No timeless realm. No anchor. Nothing to hold onto. Humans dwell in the realm of appearances dominated by the meaningless birth and death of all that exists. Motivated by the desire to prevent cruelty to self and others, Nietzche counselled opting out of the search for an ultimate meaning. Accepting the meaninglessness of life liberates humans from the manic search for answers and devaluation of the world as it is. Throughout history, literary and philosophical tracts but to a greater extent theological writings attempted to give life meaning through notions of eternity and permanence. But life and politics are essentially contingent. Following Nietzsche, they are only justified as an aesthetic phenomenon.

---

[29] For these and related themes see Jacques Derrida, "Force of Law: The 'Mystical Foundation of Authority,'" *Cardozo Law Review* Vol. 11, No. 919 (1990).
[30] See Niccolo Machiavelli, *The Prince*, translated by George Bull (New York, NY: Penguin, 2003).
[31] Friedrich Nietzsche, *The Birth of Tragedy*, translated by Walter Kaufmann (New York, NY: Vintage, 1967).
[32] Nietzsche, *The Birth of Tragedy*, 1967.

At least for Nietzsche, Greek tragedy was an important exception to otherworldly ascetism. For him, the Greek stage was an abysmal vortex that plunged the ill-fated hero into a merciless whirlpool of destruction leaving spectators contemplative, decimated, satisfied and unburdened by the cares of mundane existence.[33] Through the annihilation of the hero, tragedy freed spectators from the curse of individuation, free will and rational optimism. If life was controlled by forces outside of human control, tragedy offered a momentary release. Blinded by pride, Oedipus kills his father, has sex with his mother and then gauges his eyes out. For the audience, staring into this abyss was horrifying but also pleasurable and justified life as it is.

---

[33] Nietzsche, *The Birth of Tragedy*, 1967.

9

Joey Chestnut's self-destruction on stage is arguably tragic but with a twist. There is no "O cursed spite why was I born to set the world aright?"[34] Rather, Chestnut's mouth is the vortex into which everything sinks leaving spectators amazed and satisfied, even if only for a moment. Chestnut collapses the affective attachment to market capitalism and representative democracy by performing the disintegration of the rational self-maximizing individual upon which both depend. Chestnut's form of capitalism announces his own death and the death of God while waving the American flag on the Fourth of July. Chestnut unravels the neoliberal subject as the frenzied repetitive action of the self-work of the subject on itself. Like Oedipus, Chestnut is only an aesthetic phenomenon.

---

[34] See William Shakespeare, "The Tragedy of Hamlet, Prince of Denmark," *The Riverside Shakespeare* (Boston, MA: Houghton Mifflin Company, 1974), p. 1141-1197.

10

I searched long and hard for relevant scholarly literature to deploy as theoretical framing for Joey Chestnut. After some digging, I realized interdisciplinary work in the humanities that analyzes performance art struck me as the most relevant. According to scholars conducting research in this area, performance art opens new worlds, collapses the parameters of the present and leaves viewers with a sense of amazement and wonder.[35] For Jill Dolan, live theatrical performances are "an affective rehearsal for revolution" that allow the audience to feel what redemption might be like.[36] For Murray Edelman, "art helps counter banal political forms and so can be a liberating form of political expression."[37] However, disruptive performatives that challenge the aesthetic and intellectual coordinates of the present tend to be events staged in art galleries, museums, theatres, concert halls, film festivals and other exclusive country club aesthetic locations where they do not touch mass culture and wide audiences.[38] The stage Chestnut occupies is a different one. It is not as exclusionary as the more common ticketed venues for performance art. The Nathan's event on Coney Island, New York, is free. At least for now, anyone able to get to the location can attend the event.

---

[35] See Jill Dolan, *Utopia in Performance: Finding Hope at the Theatre* (Ann Arbor, MI: University of Michigan Press, 2008). See also José Esteban Muñoz, *Cruising Utopia: The Then and There of Queer Futurity* (New York, NY: New York University Press, 2009).
[36] See Jill Dolan, *Utopia in Performance: Finding Hope at the Theatre* (Ann Arbor, MI: University of Michigan Press, 2008), pp. 7-8.
[37] See Murray Edelman, *Constructing the Political Spectacle* (Chicago, IL: University of Chicago Press, 1988), p. 126.
[38] See Michael J. Shapiro, *Cinematic Geopolitics*, (New York, NY: Routledge, 2009) and *Punctuations: How the Arts Think the Political* (Durham, NC: Duke University Press, 2019). See also Muñoz, *Cruising Utopia,* 2009. Punk rock bands with populist appeal and openness to amateurs constitutes an exception to this claim.

In the discipline of political science, the scholarship on the politics of performance art tends to stay within established parameters for reflecting on politics construed as activism. Aesthetic phenomenon without a clear political take away tend to be ignored.[39] When it comes to performance art, there is thus a tendency to look to a narrow range of sources as objects of analysis. The political take-aways tend to operate within accepted and conventional pathways for reflection on democratic citizenship. Democratic citizenship is normally construed as the attempt "to make a difference," "do democracy" as opposed to making a mess, ruining things and causing chaos. This arguably explains why competitive eating events and hotdog eating contests have been overlooked by political scientists. Joey Chestnut exists outside of conventional understandings of politics.

Nevertheless, forty thousand people flock to Coney Island, NY to watch the hot dog eating contest every year. Nearly two million viewers in the US and internationally tune in on ESPN to watch the event on television. Based on popular fascination and interest with the event, an interrogation of the cultural and political stakes of this event strikes me as worth undertaking. A college graduate with a degree in engineering and construction management, Chestnut violates bourgeois propriety, hygiene and self-care. He deploys himself as an object for bodily vandalism. He is an engineer of his own demise. He does not eat because he is hungry. He thus calls the biological imperative to eat into question. His tempo is manic, frenzied.[40] Chestnut stages a "form of revolt that has no relation whatsoever to the laws, categories and values it would contest and ideally destroy."[41]

---

[39] See Mark Mattern and Nancy Love, Eds., *Doing Democracy: Activist Art and Cultural Politics* (Albany, NY: State University of New York Press, 2014): "To what degree can activists harness the arts and popular culture to shatter hegemony and challenge elite power?" p. 4.

[40] See Linda Williams, *Hard Core: Power, Pleasure and the 'Frenzy of the Visible,'* 1989.

[41] See Leo Bersani, *Homos* (Cambridge, MA: Harvard University Press, 1995), 152.

In terms of specific publications on Chestnut, I quickly learned that the literature on Joey Chestnut is spotty. *Hungry for Glory: The Joey Chestnut Story* offers a descriptive account of Chestnut's entrance into the world of competitive eating. The book tends to dwell on the surface, lists contests and eschews deeper analysis. *The Life and Legacy of Joey Chestnut* is a bit better but still lacks deeper connections and any theoretical insights.[42] Ryan Nerz's *Eat this Book* and Jason Fagone's *The Horseman of the Esophagus* are better in terms of charting the development of competitive eating but both avoid the types of connections I make to politics.[43] To acquire a deeper understanding of Chestnut, it is necessary to bridge the gulf between low brow popular culture and academic theory.

---

[42] Jonathan Johnson, *The Life and Legacy of Joey Chestnut: The Inside Story of a Man Who Became a Millionaire Through Competitive Eating* (North Haven, CT: Jonathan Johnson, 2023); James Brown, *Hungry for Glory,* 2024.

[43] Ryan Nerz, *Eat this Book: A Year of Gorging and Glory on the Competitive Eating Circuit* (New York, NY: St. Martin's Press, 2006). See Jason Fagone, *The Horseman of the Esophagus: Competitive Eating and the Big Fat American Dream*, (New York, NY: Crown Press, 2006).

11

The most relevant ideas I found that connect to Chestnut are presented in this chapter. The relationship between sexuality, eating, the mouth and vomiting receives precise analysis in Michael Warner's *Publics and Counterpublics*. These are interconnections that seem pertinent to Joey Chestnut, even if Chestnut does not directly participate in the creation of a counterpublic as defined by Warner. As you may recall, a counterpublic supplies "different ways of imagining stranger sociability and its reflexivity."[44] Through the defamiliarization of being and interacting, and the suspension of rigidly instrumental ways of living, a path is illuminated for the generalized transformation of public life via new and unexpected forms of contact and intimacy. In the daily life world of a capitalist society, individuals rarely encounter each other in ways that put into question boundaries between self and other. I stand here. You are over there. Even if we stand in line at Starbuck's together, we never exchange anything more than an awkward and blank stare. A culture of fear advises against talking to strangers. Life becomes an affair of profound loneliness punctuated by a competitive frenzy for scarce resources at Costco followed by a retreat into the surveillance fortress called home.

Loneliness is not destiny. Intimacy bridges distance and divisions between self and other. Intimacy with others promises communion via touch and shared experiences of ecstasy. Under capitalism, neoliberalism and patriarchy, sex is drained of its revolutionary potential and becomes a form of disconnection. Sex as disconnection is a lonely place where a limited range of actions involving genitals (e.g., phallic penetration of the vagina) and positions (e.g., doggy; missionary) constitute sex. Two people are close physically yet so far away. As a political project, Foucault redirected analysis of sexuality away from genitals and to the ear and the mouth where confession and discourse about pleasure situated intimacy in the realms of biopower and normalization. Even

---

[44] Michael Warner, *Publics and Counterpublics* (New York, NY: Zone Books, 2005), p. 122 (emphasis added).

though he did not specifically name the practices he had in mind, Foucault flagged the body and envisioned non-normative forms of pleasure as important sites of resistance.[45] His history of sexuality was a critique of its subjugation to disciplinary institutions via categorization, normalization and regulation. Foucault's goal was the reinvention the body as a site for pleasure. His broader humanist goal was experimentation with the possibilities of ecstatic disruption.

Pleasure could create alternative worlds. Alternative modes of being and living can intensify love of life and others. A powerful example of the disruption of these boundaries is provided by Michael Warner. Warner recounts a food and drink-gorging performance he experienced as a spectator in a New York, NY bar with academic colleagues. This example allows us to illuminate interrelationships between Joey Chestnut, Foucault's critique of sexuality as discipline and the utopian potential of performance art. Let's listen to Michael Warner:

> A boy, twentyish, very skateboard, comes on the low stage at one end of the bar, wearing Lycra shorts and a dog collar. He sits loosely in a restraining chair. His partner, the vomiting top, comes out and tilts the bottom's head up to the ceiling, stretching out his throat. Behind them is an array of foods. The top begins pouring milk down the boy's throat, then food, then more milk. It spills over, down his chest and onto the floor. A dynamic is established between them in which they carefully keep at the *threshold of gagging*. The bottom struggles to keep taking in more than he really can. The top is careful to give him just enough to stretch his capacities. From time to time, a baby bottle is offered as a respite, but soon the rhythm intensifies. The boy's stomach is beginning to rise and pulse, almost convulsively. It is at this point that we realize we cannot leave, cannot even look away. No one can. *The crowd is transfixed* by the scene of intimacy and display, control and abandon, ferocity and abjection. *People are moaning softly with admiration, then*

---

[45] See Michel Foucault, *The History of Sexuality*, translated by Robert Hurley (New York, NY: Vintage Books, 1990).

whistling, stomping, screaming encouragements. They have pressed forward in a compact and intimate group. Finally, as the top inserts two, then three fingers in the bottom's throat, insistently offering his own stomach for the repeated climaxes, we realize that we have never seen such a display of trust and violation. We are breathless.[46]

The involuntary convulsing of the boy's body explodes the norm and exposes the narrowness of the sexual lifeworld. Analogous to Chestnut, more food and milk than he can handle is poured into the boy's mouth. On stage, the fingers of one person are inserted into the mouth of another, punctuated with a baby bottle. This example arguably connects to what Leo Bersani calls the "redemptive reinvention of sex."[47] The audience is transfixed by the involuntary convulsions of the young man's body. But there is more to this performance than this. The audience moves closer to the stage in a collective experience of wonder. For Warner, this arguably opens new vectors for community, public intimacy, sexuality and a remapping of public life. Circus acts between ferocious animals and humans made famous by Seigfried and Roy in Las Vegas, Nevada, combine violence with raw animal energy (e.g., lion taming) and tickle the death drive.[48] This food and drink gorging example harnesses involuntary bodily energy and releases it into the public sphere in a collective experience of wonder.

As described by Warner: "The crowd is transfixed." "We are breathless." The audience is no longer an aggregate of isolated frowning individuals but emerges as a new form of community, even if only for a moment. The audience "pressed forward in a compact and intimate group." The audience "moaned, whistled,

---

[46] Warner, *Publics and Counterpublics*, 2005, p. 207 (emphasis added).

[47] Leo Bersani, *"Is the Rectum a Grave?" And Other Essays* (Chicago, IL: University of Chicago Press, 2009), p. 215.

[48] For more on the death drive see Sigmund Freud, *Beyond the Pleasure Principle*, translated by James Strachey, (New York, NY: Norton, 1990).

stomped and screamed."⁴⁹ I point out Warner's discussion of this because boundaries between self and others are also disrupted, rattled and remade at the Coney Island hotdog event. Someone who was in the audience at Coney Island attests to this, raising the issue of the erotic and political significance of the hotdog eating competition that challenges the possible objection that eating sixty hotdogs in ten minutes is only nihilistic and pathological.

---

[49] For more on transgression and the carnivalesque, see Bakhtin, *Rabelais and His World*, 2009.

12

Adrienne Rose Johnson attended a Joey Chestnut Fourth of July eating contest and observed the following that arguably compares to the previous example. Rose Johnson says this in reference to Chestnut eating hotdogs: "The crowd was sick, full, triumphant together. I imagined us all living in one body, our stomachs swelling with nitrates and salt. I felt the sweat of the camera man next to me; the private drama of Joey's look of hurt and his jaws moving up and down; the hush of quiet; the heat of July on Coney Island."[50] She continues: "For the first time, I felt like I belonged." The crowd was triumphant and "lived in one body." As hard as it might be to imagine, something akin to the emergence of a counterpublic was taking place at the hotdog eating contest. Rose Johnson felt the sweat of the camera man next to her and felt "like she belonged." On stage, Joey struggled. The audience stared and was transfixed by Joey's "look of hurt." They watched with awe Joey's "jaws moving up and down."

For Sigmund Freud, eating and sex are connected. Repressed sexual appetites manifest in binge eating. To quote Freud: "The act of eating is a destruction of the object with the final aim of incorporating it, and the sexual act is an act of aggression with the purpose of the most intimate union."[51] Even if the connection between eating and sex flagged by Freud does not satisfy the components of Warner's counterpublic of improvised intimacy, the connection is nonetheless pertinent in reference to Chestnut. With Chestnut, the individualistic and competitive character of the hot dog eating contest rattles the boundaries of neoliberal subjects and creates a new world, at least for the audience that views the event in person. Rose Johnson's experience at the hotdog eating contest indicates that something unique happened there that combines the erotic character of public transgression with the act of ingesting more food than one needs and can handle. Chestnut's masculinity is

---

[50] See Adrienne Rose Johnson, "The Art of Competitive Eating," *Gastronomica*, 16:3 (Fall 2016), p. 113.

[51] See Sigmund Freud, *An Outline of Psychoanalysis*, translated by James Strachey, (New York, NY: Norton, 1989).

performed and proven via his discomfort and self-sacrifice for a cause greater than himself. He pleases and satisfies the audience without touching them. He defiles himself but with pain, not lust.

It is important to note as a point of contrast to the vomiting performance in NYC, Chestnut does not vomit and is alone as a competitor on stage. He feeds himself hot dogs in buns as a solitary act. If he had a partner on stage that gently fed him one hot dog after another, sometimes two at a time, then giving him a baby bottle, then putting fingers in his mouth to fit more dogs inside, while slowly pushing Chestnut beyond his physical constraints, a counterpublic would arguably emerge that would satisfy Michael Warner's definition. The counterpublic would put into question the artificial divisions constituted by a political culture based on abstract and decontextualized individuals. It would also put into question the norms of heteronormative sex culture where narrow limits are imposed on affection and intimacy. The broader point that is pertinent here is the visceral and visual dimension of eros construed outside of the heteronormative reproductive sex matrix. When intimacy appears in public in ways that disrupt propriety and exceed the matrix of sex in the bourgeois suburban private realm, artificial boundaries are shattered. New types of connections with others become possible. Consciousness of one's place, self and location with others are transformed. The world is remade, if even for a moment.[52]

---

[52] For the politically transformative character of public sex see Samuel R. Delaney, *Times Square Red, Times Square Blue*, (New York, NY: New York University Press, 1999).

13

There are other worlds. This is precisely the point made by Saidiya Hartman in her book about how marginalized groups live, love, survive and thrive otherwise. In her discussion of experimental and public sex in *Wayward Lives, Beautiful Experiments*, Hartman describes the events at 80 Edgecombe Avenue, an address in Harlem, New York. For Hartman, public sex and moments of collective intimacy have anarchistic transformative power:

> The public sex and collective lovemaking, like the environment, were beautiful, worldly-wise, and testimony to a distinctly modern life. In the elegant flat, the sharp edge of pleasure, the moans, whispers, and laughter blanketing the room, the choked breath of orgasm *shattered the boundaries of the self*, effaced the lines of social division, unmade men and women. *The utter dissolution of the bounded, discrete self was the gift*. The gay rebels and the gender queers savored the lush refuge; welcomed the opportunity to jettison propriety. *Guests mingled across the divide of class and race, strangers became intimates*, an English aristocrat fell in love with a Negro actress.[53]

Hartman flags important aspects of the dissolution of boundaries that lead to the creation of a new world including the disintegration of the bordered self, cross class intimacy, creation of new connections, laughter and orgasm. Proper boundaries were transgressed: "An English aristocrat fell in love with a Negro actress." Institutions of social reproduction were shattered. People entered "with a husband and exited with a wife."[54] Property and propriety were joyfully abandoned. Mine and thine were no longer

---

[53] See Saidiya Hartman, *Wayward Lives, Beautiful Experiments: Intimate Histories of Riotous Black Girls, Troublesome Women, and Queer Radicals* (New York, NY: Norton, 2019), pp. 323-4, (emphasis added).
[54] Hartman, *Wayward Lives*, 2019, p. 322.

distinct. The participants practiced "a certain refusal of sex as we know it."[55]

Like Nietzsche's discussion of Dionysian excess and loss of the boundaries of the self in *The Birth of Tragedy*, Hartman too justifies life as an aesthetic phenomenon (e.g., "making living an art").[56] The constraints preventing the ecstatic dissolution of selves ran deeper for Hartman, though. In Harlem, daily life was punctuated by blocked opportunities and lynch mob horror as the normal practices of the police and actual mobs. In Harlem, a racialized space constituted by American apartheid, people were piled up on each other and were never meant to survive. Individuals were constituted as criminals by birth and appearance, always already guilty, hopelessly pathological, incapable of transformation by the helping hands of a benevolent, Christian and paternalistic white society. But within the chaos, noise and terror, as Hartman demonstrates via archival research, new forms of beauty and life emerged. For Hartman, unlike for W. E. B. Du Bois, the black mass and street anarchy was beautiful, wild and reckless. Noise, trash and jazz flooded the streets. Street level anarchy dissolved categories that pinned people to predetermined roles. Anarchy and noise collapsed the past, trashed norms and opened "other ways to live."[57] Du Bois's top-down social scientific gaze acquired at Harvard University from 1888 to 1895 only permitted him to see hopelessness and pathology in the face of the black mass.[58]

Hartman sees something beautiful and sublime in the same face. Namely, the fierce refusal to be dominated in everyday life. For Hartman, this rebellion and refusal opened new ways of being, living, loving, flying and soaring. Soaring occurred in alleys, on the street, in bars and clubs and in the flat at 80 Edgecomb Avenue. The black mass was unassimilable and ungovernable. For too long they

---

[55] Bersani, "Is the Rectum a Grave?" 2009, p. 215.

[56] Hartman, *Wayward Lives*, 2019, xiv.

[57] Hartman, *Wayward Lives*, 2019, xv.

[58] See W. E. B. Du Bois, *The Philadelphia Negro: A Social Study and History of Pennsylvania's Black American Population; their Education, Environment and Work* (New York, NY: Pantianos Classics, 1899).

were enslaved people. Controlled and pinched economically, politically, sexually, socially and culturally. For Negroes in Harlem, anarchy facilitated "living otherwise" and being "at war with the given."[59] The refusal to be governed allowed "experiments in freedom."[60] Patriotism was not on anyone's mind.

---

[59] Hartman, *Wayward Lives*, 2019, pp. 33, 107.
[60] Hartman, *Wayward Lives*, 2019, p. 17.

14

Even though the hotdog competition takes place on the Fourth of July, Chestnut does not strike me as patriotic in any obvious way. Chestnut does many of the things a good patriotic American is told to do including being a consumer, a brand, an entrepreneur and a spectacle. In that regard, he is not that different from members of the Kardashian family. In *Patriotism and Other Mistakes*, George Kateb defines patriotism as love of one's country and "a readiness to die and to kill for what is largely a figment of the imagination."[61] For Kateb, patriotism is masculinist and "disposed to disregard morality."[62] With chest puffed out and stern facial expression, the masculine male asserts his will, takes charge and expects deference. The threat of violence backs up the swagger.[63] Traditional masculinity is a violent military project, a way of "occupying public space."[64] Chestnut's masculinity and patriotism are paradoxical.[65] Taking in more than anyone else can handle, Chestnut consumes public space by filling his mouth with hotdogs, gulps and groans, then chokes it all down. He doesn't pursue happiness but eats it. His consumption is measured and simultaneously excessive. Chestnut celebrates himself and America via self-negation but without a national swagger.[66] For the Princeton

---

[61] George Kateb, *Patriotism and Other Mistakes* (New Haven, CT: Yale University Press, 2006), p. 8.

[62] Kateb, *Patriotism and Other Mistakes*, 2006, p. 9.

[63] On the relationship between masculinity and violence, see bell hooks, *The Will to Change: Men, Masculinity and Love*, (New York, NY: Washington Square Press, 2004).

[64] Warner, *Publics and Counterpublics*, 2005, p. 24.

[65] On the links between masculinity, self-torture and violence to others see bell hooks, *The Will to Change*, 2004.

[66] The United States ranks 10th in the world in terms of obesity, with 41.64% of the population suffering from this affliction. Discussions about obesity, nutrition, dieting and exercise are common on televisual and internet media outlets. Connections between obesity and mental health reflect a neoliberal calculus regime for the contemporary subject. Despite the serious health risks obesity poses

University political theorist Kateb, everyone is a patriot "of some kind and to some degree."[67] Temper it, moderate it, Kateb seems to say. In lieu of patriotism, Kateb promotes "the art of living with oneself."[68] Joey Chestnut's patriotism is a strange form of self-sacrifice and of living with himself poorly. He is arguably a bad role model for children. He is not a hunger artist as depicted in Franz Kafka's story but a bloated one. The *Oxford English Dictionary* defines bloated as "of the body, face, etc." "Swollen, puffed up, turgid." The "effect of gluttony and self-indulgence."[69]

---

including diabetes and hypertension, there is no sign that American binge eating will end anytime soon. See https://data.worldobesity.org/rankings/ (accessed April 16, 2024).
[67] Kateb, *Patriotism and Other Mistakes*, 2006.
[68] Kateb, *Patriotism and Other Mistakes*, 2006, p. 20.
[69] *The Compact Edition of the Oxford English Dictionary* (Oxford, UK: Oxford University Press, 1971), p. 232.

15

It could be objected that there is nothing redeeming about Joey Chestnut. That he is disgusting and represents a low point in the country, weakens the critical intellectual spirit and is a national embarrassment. That Chestnut is nothing more than a bad spectacle. And that apathy and indifference to real political issues like healthcare is likely to be exacerbated by the distraction called Joey Chestnut.[70] That Chestnut is a sign of this country circling the drain. That Chestnut gives us a Fourth of July without Frederick Douglass and a day filled with meaninglessness and stupidity.

Additionally, the comparison between competitive hotdog contests and pornography could be viewed as silly. The obvious difference is this. Hotdog eating lacks a "money shot," meaning, an ejaculating penis, grimacing face and convulsing torso. Even if someone vomits during the hot dog eating event, this is a categorically different act compared to ejaculation. Also, ingesting a hotdog is different from *fellatio*. No pleasure is given to the hotdog while it is in Chestnut's mouth because hotdogs are inanimate objects. Finally, the point of porn is to sexually arouse viewers. Viewers of a hotdog eating competition may watch the event with a certain level of fascination but not sexual arousal.

During the Spring 2024 semester, I asked the students in my American government course what they thought about Chestnut and whether they thought he was engaged in a form of civil disobedience. One student said he does not challenge anything. Another said that he was solely entertainment. Another wrote that he was not contesting an unjust law and that he does not advocate change. Another wrote that he is not connected to a social or political issue. That he lacks a clear political and social agenda. That he does not challenge power structures. That the event was backed by a

---

[70] For these and related themes see Nina Eliasoph, *Avoiding Politics: How Americans Produce Apathy in Everyday Life*, (New York, NY: Cambridge University Press, 1998).

corporation and is only about making money. Most of my students stated that Chestnut was not being political.[71] I respectfully disagree.

From the vantage point of an intellectual troublemaker, Joey Chestnut is a strange form of political and utopian light peering out at us from the horizon. People watch him eat because there is something beautifully unusual about what he does. He takes us out of our comfort zone. He takes himself beyond limits and lives on to eat at another competition. From the right vantage point, every hotdog Chestnut eats is analogous to a wrung on the ladder to utopia. As he eats one and then two, he ascends upward to the promised land. Each hotdog is cradled like a baby bird in Chestnut's hands, flaps its wings, and then flies into his mouth. Chestnut thus models an antipolitics. He shows us how to "decline to participate in any sociality at all."[72] Chestnut's hot dog gorging is a way to refuse all options by devouring all of them. It is a way to collapse emotional attachment to the social and political status quo through the public display of irrelevance, irreverence and overturning hierarchies. Chestnut announces the death of God after the death of God via shoveling hotdogs into his mouth and down his throat. As with porn, Chestnut is the fantasy of a better future. He is just as empty as American politics, an organized system designed to prevent anything that benefits ordinary people from happening. Chestnut shows us how a seemingly inconsequential and pointless public spectacle can push America to a new rock bottom, and open vectors for political reflection. Chestnut forces us to come to terms with low brow utopian performance art as an antipolitics. By antipolitics, I mean the refusal of the available options for political engagement. You don't have to be a political scientist to realize that politics isn't pretty, rational and a space for hope. That doesn't mean it cannot be funny. As Chestnut eats one hotdog and then another, I can hear the faint sound of Iggy Pop's song "I wanna be your dog." If Chestnut ran for political office, he would probably win. If Chestnut can eat sixty-two hotdogs in ten minutes, anything is possible.

---

[71] The students were in my Spring 2024 POSC 2305 US Federal Government and Politics course at the University of Texas Rio Grande Valley.
[72] See Leo Bersani, *Homos*, 1995, p. 168.

CONCLUSION

The punk rock band called "Upchuck" mixes delinquency, street skate culture and protest punk to create a dissonant aesthetic of musical disruption that elevates, liberates and irritates.[73] As US politics sinks to new lows and circles the drain, join me in celebrating Joey Chestnut's America. As difficult as this might be to accept, Joey Chestnut represents the triumph of American democracy. If you are going to defend democracy, be prepared to crawl in the gutter. Trump did. The path forward is not to bemoan right wing extremists, take the train called pessimism, and step off in negative land. The path forward can be found in a critical queer theory of the hot dog. This manifests as a call for thousands of comedic, futile and stupid nihilistic acts that crash the political and economic status quo and mobilize the people via laughter for new modes of agency. Joey Chestnut's America is an invitation to make trouble, overturn hierarchies, fart in public, laugh out loud, and disrupt conventional paths for reflecting on democracy.[74] Finally, celebrating Chestnut is a way to come to terms with the stupidity of American politics without losing one's sense of humor.

---

[73] See https://upchuckatl.bandcamp.com/ (accessed August 26, 2024).

[74] See John Waters, *Make Trouble* (Chapel Hill, NC: Algonquin Books, 2017).

ACKNOWLEDGEMENTS

I thank Marcelo Hoffman, Katherine Young, Esteban O. Brown, Michael Liscomb, Bryant Sculos, Jennifer Leigh Disney, Rudy Leal McCormack, Bradley J. Macdonald, William L. Niemi and Robert Rowe for conversations pertaining to this project and/or comments on an earlier draft. I thank the anonymous readers of this manuscript for helpful feedback. I thank my students and political science colleagues at the University of Texas Rio Grande Valley for a vibrant intellectual environment. For research assistance, I thank Hannya Flores, Leslie Reyes and Sofia Zamora Wiley. I also thank Dongkyu Kim, department chair, and José Dávila-Montes, Dean, College of Liberal Arts. At a more personal level, I thank my partner Kerry for enduring many conversations about this book. I thank my mother Nadja P. Sokoloff for her kindness and support.

William W. Sokoloff, 2025

William W. Sokoloff was born in Whittier, California. He was an undergraduate at California State University, Long Beach and completed his graduate work at the University of Massachusetts, Amherst. He is the author of *Confrontational Citizenship: Reflections on Hatred, Rage, Revolution and Revolt* (SUNY, 2017) and *Political Science Pedagogy: A Critical, Radical and Utopian Perspective* (Palgrave, 2020). He also co-edited *Tactics and Emancipation in the Age of Authoritarian Neoliberalism* (Routledge, 2023). He teaches in the Department of Political Science at the University of Texas, Rio Grande Valley. He lives in McAllen, Texas and the west side of San Antonio, Texas.

THE DIVERS COLLECTION

Number 1
Hôtel des Étrangers, poems by Joachim Sartorius translated from German by Scott J. Thompson

Number 2
Making Art, a memoir by Mary Julia Klimenko

Number 3
XISLE, a novel by Tamsin Spencer Smith

Number 4
Famous Dogs of the Civil War, a novel by Ben Dunlap

Number 5
Now Let's See What You're Gonna Do, poetry by Katarina Gogou translated from Greek to English by A.S. with an introduction by Jack Hirschman

Number 6
Sunshine Bell / The Autobiography of a Genius, an annotated edition by Ben Dunlap

Number 7
The Profound M: found photos paired with poems by Tamsin Spencer Smith with an introduction by Matt Gonzalez

Number 8
The Glint in a Fox's Eye & Other Revelations, volume one of a three-part memoir by Ben Dunlap

Number 9
The Origins of Bliss, volume two of a three-part memoir by Ben Dunlap

Number 10
Proud, Open-Eyed and Laughing, volume three of a three-part memoir by Ben Dunlap

Number 11
Esmerelda's Story, a historical novella by Mary Julia Klimenko

Number 12
Private Instigator, a Journey through the Underworld of Disorganized Crime by Steve Vender

Number 13
Dreaming as One, Poetry, Poets and Community in Bolinas, California 1967-1980 by Kevin Opstedal

Number 14
Art Writings: 2008-2024 by Matt Gonzalez

Number 15
*Joey Chestnut's America:
Politics, Patriotism and the Future of Democracy by* William W. Sokoloff

THE PAGE POETS SERIES

Number 1
Between First & Second Sleep by Tamsin Spencer Smith

Number 2
The Michaux Notebook by Micah Ballard

Number 3
Sketch of the Artist by Patrick James Dunagan

Number 4
Different Darknesses by Jason Morris

Number 5
Suspension of Mirrors by Mary Julia Klimenko

Number 6
The Rise & Fall of Johnny Volume by Garrett Caples

Number 7
Used with Permission by Charlie Pendergast

Number 8
Deconfliction by Katharine Harer

Number 9
Unlikely Saviors by Stan Stone

Number 10
Beauty Will Be Convulsive by Matt Gonzalez

Number 11
Displacement Geology by Tamsin Spencer Smith

Number 12
The Public Sound by Marina Lazzara

Number 13
Record of Records by Rod Roland

Number 14
Strangers We Have Known by John Briscoe

Number 15
Cutting Teeth by Jesse Holwitz

Number 16
Other Scavengers by Lauren Caldwell

Number 17
Cueonia by Jesse Holwitz

Number 18
In the Museum of Hunting and Nature by Cynthia Randolph

Number 19
A New Species of Color by Tamsin Spencer Smith

Number 20
Busy Secret by Micah Ballard

Number 21
Out of the Blue by Fran Carbonaro

Number 22
Broadway Azaleas by Sunnylyn Thibodeaux

Number 23
War News II by Beau Beausoleil

Number 24
Hailstones by Justin Robinson

Number 25
Exile on Beach Street by Kevin Opstedal

www.ingramcontent.com/pod-product-compliance
Lightning Source LLC
Chambersburg PA
CBHW051704040426
42446CB00009B/1297